Thinking STORIES

by

Nadine Webb

First Printing: 2018

Copyright © 2018 by Nadine Webb
All rights reserved.

Printed in the United Kingdom.

All rights reserved. This book or any of its parts may not be reproduced or used in any manner whatsoever without the express written permission of the author and publisher. However, brief quotations in a book review or scholarly journal are permitted.
Authors and their publications mentioned in this work and bibliography have their copyright protection. All brand and product names used in this book are trademarks, registered trademarks, or trade names and belong to the respective owners.
The author is unassociated with any product or vendor in this book.

About the author

Nadine Webb has been a school teacher since 2003 and has taken part in hundreds of assemblies. She has witnessed amazing transformations and great initiatives taken by pupils who got inspired by wonderful stories. In turn she wants to inspire more generations of pupils in order to make a better world with more mature, well-balanced and generous people.

Introduction

This book will cover most situations that can happen in a child's life and inspire them to become more caring, confident, grateful and much more. Every school should share these enthralling and memorable stories.

Contents

1. Everyone has a gift 5
2. Time is the best gift 9
3. Keep your options open 13
4. Do not burn bridges 17
5. Be proud of who you are 21
6. One person's banter is another person's bullying . 25
7. Don't be afraid to be honest 29
8. Try to the best of your ability 33
9. Don't judge by appearances 37
10. Prepare for the best nights out 41
11. Report bullying 45
12. Know your strengths – don't be swayed by others 49
13. Treat people kindly 53
14. Take time to listen to older people 57
15. Those who shout loudest aren't always right 61
16. Everything in moderation 65
17. Respect people's time 69
18. Try new things – you might discover a new talent 73
19. Be yourself – don't always try to fit in 77
20. Don't be afraid to admit mistakes 81
21. Don't judge people by money or possessions 85
22. Not everyone tells the truth 89
23. If people gossip to you, they probably gossip about you as well 93
24. Don't invent things to get attention 97
25. Be patient with others 101
26. Be kind to animals 105

1
Everyone has a gift

It was the day of the play, and Ms Wilkes strode into the school with nervous determination. Her year nine drama class had been rehearsing for weeks. All of the class had wanted a part in the play except for one girl, Jasmine. However much Ms Wilkes had tried to convince her to have a small part – she needn't even have a speaking role – Jasmine insisted that she was too shy and that she absolutely hated being on stage. Eventually, Ms Wilkes had agreed that she could just watch.

When Ms Wilkes reached the staffroom, she was met in the doorway by Mrs Sleemon. "I don't want to worry you," she said, "but Mr Gladwell has called in sick."

Ms Wilkes froze. Mr Gladwell was in charge of music and lighting, and all things technical. He was

5

the only one who knew how to work all the equipment. They would have to cancel.

She gloomily walked along the hall to the drama room where she was meeting the class to go through last-minute rehearsals. When she got there, the room was a buzz of excitement. Some of the kids had already got into their costumes. Others were putting face paints on each other.

"Everyone," she called, sounding angrier than she had planned. "I need your attention for a moment."

They all settled down and looked at her in surprise.

She swallowed. "I'm afraid Mr Gladwell can't be with us today, so we are going to have to cancel the play. I'm sorry, but no one else knows how to work the equipment."

There was an instant roar of disapproval from the class. Ms Wilkes could hardly look at all those disappointed faces. Then she noticed that Jasmine had come to the front and had her hand in the air.

"Yes, Jasmine?"

"I could do the music and lights."

Ms Wilkes paused. "Do you know how?"

Jasmine nodded. "I've been watching Mr Gladwell. It's not that difficult, really."

Ms Wilkes laughed. "Well, that would be amazing! Shall we have a trial run? Come on, everyone. We will run the first scene. Get into positions."

There was a buzz as 30 students moved onto the stage. Jasmine ran to the back and slipped into the technician's booth.

"Go!" Ms Wilkes shouted. The lights came up, in exactly the right order. The music blared through the speakers. She looked back at Jasmine. She was sitting with a look of concentration on her face, her brows furrowed.

They ran the whole opening scene, and everything went perfectly. Ms Wilkes shook her head, annoyed with herself: why hadn't she ever recognised Jasmine's gifts before?

Needless to say, the play was a roaring success.

THINKING STORIES

2

Time is the best gift

Ben walked to school every day, and had done for several years now. One thing that had remained constant over those years was one particular small bungalow. Every morning he glanced in through what must be the lounge window and saw a small, old lady sitting in the chair, looking out at him. She waved to him every morning. His mother had told him her name was Mrs Brown.

One morning, Ben was walking towards Mrs Brown's house when he saw the postman had left a parcel at the end of her path, beside the old mail box. Ben knew that Mrs Brown couldn't walk down to collect it, so before he got nervous and changed his mind, he picked up the box and walked up the pathway.

He glanced in at Mrs Brown and held up the parcel to show her what he was doing. She smiled, gave a little wave, and then eased herself out of the chair.

Ben got to the front door and waited a couple of minutes for Mrs Brown to get there. When she opened it, she was leaning on a zimmer frame. She was even smaller than he'd imagined she would be.

"Oh, thank you, dear," said Mrs Brown. "I think we must have a new postman. He doesn't know to bring it up to the door."

Ben smiled. "Would you like me to bring it inside?"

"Yes please, dear. That is, if you're sure you have time." Mrs Brown shuffled backwards a foot to allow Ben to walk past her into the lounge.

The room was small and simple but there was a large vase of flowers on the mantelpiece.

"Nice flowers," said Ben.

"Yes, my daughter sent those. It's my birthday, you see," she said.

"Oh! Happy birthday!" said Ben. He glanced down at the box. "Is this a birthday present?"

Mrs Brown peered at the return label on the box. "Yes, it looks like it's from my son," she said. "Could you open it, please? My hands aren't very good these days."

Ben placed the box down on the coffee table and pulled off the tape. He opened the flaps of the box. "Wow!" he said. "It's an iPad!"

He looked at Mrs Brown, expecting her to be as excited as he was. But her face was sad.

"My daughter sent me a DVD player as well."

"Your son and daughter must really love you to send these incredible gifts."

Mrs Brown shook her head. "I don't ever see them," she said. "They're very busy people. I don't need any of these gifts. I don't even know how to use them. I'd far rather hear what they've been doing, how my grandchildren are."

Ben looked down at the iPad, unsure of what to say.

"Oh, listen to me, going on," said Mrs Brown, brightening. "Thank you for coming in. You've really made my day."

Ben turned towards the front door. As he opened it, he turned back around. "I can teach you how to use the iPad," said Ben. "And the DVD player. If you'd like?"

Mrs Brown looked surprised. "Really?" she said. "I would love that. Yes please."

Ben smiled. "I'll come over after school."

3
Keep your options open

"I know you can do this, Simon," said Mr Randall. "You just need to focus until the exams are over."

Simon shrugged. "It's all a waste of time anyway."

Simon was in his final year at school, and his exams were coming up. He had already decided that he wanted to work on his father's farm after school, so he wasn't bothered about doing well. He was only taking the exams because he had to.

"I know that you don't see this as important," said Mr Randall, "and working on your dad's farm sounds like a great plan. But it's always good to have other options."

The bell went shortly afterwards, signalling the end of the school day. As Simon walked home, he imagined his future. He would be outside, working the fields, probably driving the tractor or herding the sheep. No more stuffy classrooms, no more pieces of paper, and certainly no more maths.

When Simon got home, his father was sitting in his office, his head in his hands. He looked up as his son entered the room. "Simon, I'm glad you're home."

"What's the matter, Dad?"

"I've just been to the bank. The farm's in trouble."

Simon's heart started to race. "What sort of trouble?"

"It's not making money. It's breaking my heart, but we might have to sell up, Simon."

"No, you can't," Simon said. "I'll help you. I'll work on the farm full-time."

His father shook his head. "I'm sorry, son. It's about more than just farming, nowadays. The modern farmers are all selling online, setting up shops. I have no idea how to do all that stuff."

KEEP YOUR OPTIONS OPEN

Simon paused. "I can learn to do that. Mr Randall runs extra computer classes for students interested in business."

Simon stayed up all night thinking. If only he had paid more attention in school, he could have noticed that his dad needed help. At this rate, he wasn't even going to pass maths.

The next day, Simon marched into school and went straight to Mr Randall's classroom. He found his teacher at his desk with a coffee in his hand.

"My dad might sell the farm," Simon said. "I need to pass my exams, and I need to learn how to run an online business. Can you help me?"

Mr Randall smiled. "Let's get started."

THINKING STORIES

Be Yourself and don't wait for approval

4
Do not burn bridges

Nathan had been ballet dancing since he was old enough to walk, and had won a cabinet full of trophies throughout primary school. When he started high school, though, he quickly decided that ballet wasn't cool. He came home to his mother and announced that he was giving it up.

She was shocked. "But Nathan, you've worked on it your whole life," she said. "You're so talented."

He shook his head. "Not any more," he said. "I don't want to get beaten up in the playground. I want to have friends."

"You don't have to give up ballet to achieve those things," his mother said quietly.

"Sorry, Mum," he said, "but I've decided."

Nathan went up to his bedroom and found every piece of ballet clothing that he had, put them all into a bag, and threw it into the outside bin.

The following week at school, the headteacher made an announcement. There was an inter-school talent contest coming up, and she desperately wanted the school to do well. The school had never been placed before, and she wanted students to come forward and do their school proud. Nathan sat and listened to the principal talking, knowing he could do very well for the school, if only his talent wasn't so embarrassing.

On his way home that day, he overheard a group of boys talking. One was saying to the others that he wished they could enter, but that his mother had never let him join any clubs or learn anything outside of school.

Nathan suddenly felt very guilty. His mother had dedicated her life to funding his ballet, driving him around to classes and competitions, and he had thrown it all away. Literally.

His mum was in the kitchen when he got home. "I could have represented the school, Mum," he said. "But I gave up the one thing I've ever been good at, and chucked all my stuff away."

She smiled at him, then turned to rummage through the cupboard under the sink. "It's never too late," she said, handing him the bag of ballet clothes that he had thrown away. "Show them what you're made of."

THINKING STORIES

5
Be proud of who you are

Ellie enjoyed school and she had a good group of friends, but she never felt like she totally fitted in. The three other girls she hung around with – Amber, Katherine and Stella – all came from well-off families. They lived in large houses in the country, and tended to wear designer clothes. Ellie, on the other hand, came from a family who didn't have much money. Her parents both worked long hours, but they lived in a small terraced house on the edge of town, and most of her clothes were from cheap shops. Some were even second hand.

Over the past year, since starting at high school, Ellie had been to each of her friends' houses, but she hadn't invited them back to hers. She was too embarrassed and worried that they would think she wasn't worth being friends with.

21

One Friday after school, Ellie and her three friends walked into town to go to the cinema. When they got there, though, it turned out that they had got the timings wrong and they had missed the film.

"Can we go to your place?" Katherine asked Ellie.

"Erm, can't we go to yours?" Ellie said.

"My parents don't get home until late," she said.

Amber and Stella also had similar problems.

"Please, Ellie," said Katherine, "It's cold out here and we've got nothing to do. We promise to be good and not embarrass you in front of your parents!"

If only they knew, Ellie thought, that it was quite the other way around. As they walked towards her end of town, Ellie's three friends chatted happily, but she hardly spoke the whole way. She was so worried that this would be the end of the friendship. By tomorrow, her house with no carpets and only two small bedrooms would be the talk of the class, and everyone would laugh at her.

Once they reached the front door, Ellie glanced over her shoulder, expecting looks of shock or even disgust, but the others were still just laughing and talking and, well, being *normal*. She put her key in the lock and pushed the door open, and they all walked in.

BE PROUD OF WHO YOU ARE

Ellie's mum had just got in from work, and was putting her coat on the hook in the hallway. "Oh hello, sweetie. You've brought your friends – great!"

Ellie cringed. Why did her mum have to be so embarrassing?

Katherine stepped past her and introduced herself. Amber and Stella did the same. Ellie's mum ushered them all into the lounge and then fetched lemonade and cake for everyone. Ellie watched her friends being polite and grateful, and her mum being generous and fun, and she started to relax. For the next hour, the five of them chatted and ate cake.

When it was time for the other three to meet their parents and go home, Ellie saw them out of the front door. Stella turned to her and said, "Why have we never met your mum before? She's so cool!"

Ellie grinned and waved her friends off as they walked up the road and disappeared around the corner. She went back into her home, realising that the only thing embarrassing about her life was her inability to see how great it was.

THINKING STORIES

NEVER

BE BULLIED INTO SILENCE. NEVER ALLOW YOURSELF
TO BE MADE A VICTIM.
ACCEPT NO ONE'S DEFINITION OF YOUR LIFE, BUT
DEFINE YOURSELF

6

One person's banter is another person's bullying

Sayma, Neeve and Rachel all lined up, ready to start netball practice. Mrs Richards, their P.E. teacher, was standing in front of them, sorting out the tabards.

Now in Year Ten, the three girls had been friends since primary school. They were chatting about this and that when Theresa, another girl from their primary school, joined the line behind them.

Sayma grinned and nudged Rachel. "You'd better hope Theresa isn't on your team. We all remember what happened in Year Five."

"Oh yeah," said Rachel, and turned to Theresa. "Did you bring your spare underwear today, just in case?"

The three friends giggled. Theresa looked down at the floor.

Another girl overheard them. "Did you wet yourself, Theresa?" She laughed. "Did the ball scare you?"

Theresa's face was red. "No," she muttered. "I was laughing."

The girls sniggered again.

Mrs Richards came over to where they were standing. "Girls, that's enough," she said, to Sayma and Rachel in particular.

"It's only banter, Miss," said Sayma. "Theresa found it funny too, at the time."

"One person's banter," said Mrs Richards, "is another person's bullying."

Theresa said nothing.

The next day, Theresa didn't turn up to netball practice. In fact, the girls didn't see her until the following Monday when Sayma bumped into her in the corridor.

"All right, Ther?" Sayma said. "Richards gave me a right going over when you didn't show up to netball last week. She said I had bullied you!" She laughed.

One Person's Banter...

"That thing in netball," said Theresa, her face serious, "was four years ago. I know it was funny at the time, but I don't want it brought up constantly in front of new people. It's really embarrassing for me."

Sayma paused. "I guess I didn't think…"

"What if I had said stuff about you?" Theresa interrupted. "What if I'd brought up the time you tripped over and ended up sitting on the lunchtime supervisor's lap? Or the time you pretended to faint because you fancied the headmaster?"

Theresa lifted her bag onto her shoulder and walked away down the corridor. Sayma resolved to think more carefully about banter in the future.

THINKING STORIES

7

Don't be afraid to be honest

Ashley was sitting at his desk in English class, listening to Ms Sadana talk about the upcoming prize-giving day.

"I need someone to make a speech on behalf of the year. A lot of students, staff and parents will be there, so it's quite a big deal. I need someone who will take it seriously. Ashley, I was wondering if maybe you'd like to do it?"

Ashley looked up, shocked. He couldn't imagine anything worse. He met Ms Sadana's smiling eyes. Then he looked around – all his classmates were staring at him. "Erm, yes, okay," he said.

Ms Sadana tilted her head to one side. "Are you sure? You don't have to do it if you'd rather not…"

"No, no, I'd love to." Ashley forced a smile. "Great."

Her face relaxed. "Wonderful," she said. "I think you'll do a brilliant job."

As Ashley left the classroom, he wondered what on earth he had done. He hated even reading out in class, let alone making a speech in front of the whole school and their parents. But all those eyes had been on him, and he didn't want to let them down, especially Ms Sadana. He would just have to do it.

The following week was the most stressful of Ashley's life. He hardly slept, barely ate, and almost every waking moment was spent fretting about the speech. He had written it and re-written it five times, but still wasn't happy with it. The lack of sleep meant that he couldn't concentrate in school and he started to forget to do homework. Teachers started to comment on it: "What's going on with you, Ashley?"; "Is everything okay?"; "Are you unwell?"

To every question, Ashley replied that he was fine, smiled, and apologised, insisting that he would try harder.

Two days before prize-giving, Ms Sadana called Ashley to her office. When he arrived, with a pale face and big dark rings under his eyes, she shook her head. "Ashley, I'm so sorry."

"What for, Miss?"

"For asking you to do this speech. This is what all this is about, isn't it? You are dreading it."

Ashley thought about protesting but realised he didn't have the energy. Instead, he looked at the floor.

"Why on earth didn't you say so?" Ms Sadana said. "There are plenty of other students who would love to do it."

Ashley looked up into her face. "Really?"

"Yes!" she laughed. "I just wanted to give you the chance first."

"Oh!" he said, and smiled genuinely for the first time in days.

"I'll ask someone else today, and we will say no more about it. Now you can get some sleep and actually look forward to prize-giving day!"

THINKING STORIES

> **Don't** start because it's easy. **Start** because it's **worth** trying. **Don't** stop because it's **hard**. **Stop** because you've tried your **Best**.

8
Try to the best of your ability

Ibrihim was in his history class, and the teacher, Mrs Maxwell, had just finished detailing their project for the following week. In groups of four, they had to deliver a presentation on any aspect of the Second World War. Ibrihim was pleased as he found the Second World War interesting. Mrs Maxwell drew names out of a hat to decide which groups people would be in.

Ibrihim was with Jessica, Lei and Connor. He didn't know any of them particularly well. The class stood up and rearranged themselves so that they were in their designated groups.

As soon as they'd sat down, Jessica took control. She whipped out a pad and pen, and wrote down prospective topics for their presentation. Ibrihim put forward a few ideas, as did Lei. Connor said nothing, but occasionally nodded along with an idea. Jessica read the list that they had created, and then declared that they should do her idea: "Ambulance Drivers" was the best and they would do that. Ibrihim was mildly irked that they hadn't made the decision together, but he let it go.

Next, Jessica started giving orders for who should do which part. "I think I should do the introduction and conclusion, as it was my idea and I know a lot about it."

Ibrihim wasn't about to challenge her; it didn't mean enough to him. Frankly, he was getting worried that Connor wasn't going to do anything at all. He still hadn't spoken. Ibrihim suggested that Connor researched and wrote the section about how the ambulance crews were organised. Connor nodded again.

The following week, it was the day of Ibribim's presentation. He had researched some case studies of ambulance drivers and had written a report about what life was like for them and what atrocities they saw. When he arrived at the classroom, Connor and Lei were already there. The three of them read each other's work. They were just about done when Jessica turned up.

"Hey guys," she said, and then she caught sight of their presentations. "Oh, is that today?" she said, her eyes too wide to be believable. "I completely forgot!"

Ibrihim stared at her. "You knew it was today, Jessica. You wrote it all down in our notes last week."

"Oh, it'll be okay," she said. "I'll just read out a part of yours instead."

"No, you won't," said Ibrihim. "We've all worked hard on ours."

Ibrihim found Mrs Maxwell and explained what had happened. He, Lei and Connor delivered the presentation, and they received an A grade. Jessica sat at the back of the class, scowling throughout.

THINKING STORIES

9

Don't judge by appearances

It was a new academic year at Sidwell School. Chris was now in Year Ten, which was good. He had become bored with Year Nine. He walked into his form room and sat down in his usual place. His two best friends, Xiao and Kenny, were already there and waiting for him. Kenny looked excited.

"There's a new guy in our form," he said. "His name's Jack, and he's a champion motocross rider."

Chris could see why Kenny was so keen. He loved motorbikes, especially motocross, but his mum refused to buy him one. They were too dangerous, she'd said.

"He's pretty cool," Kenny continued. He was almost gushing now. "He wears designer trainers and everything."

"There he is," Xiao whispered, nodding towards the door.

Chris turned around and he could see what Kenny meant. He *did* look cool, though Chris would never have said it out loud. He had dark hair, almost jet black, and it sort of swept across his forehead. He looked like the type that all the girls were going to fancy, but this was another thought that Chris would definitely be keeping to himself.

"You should go and talk to him, Ken," Xiao said. "Maybe he'll let you ride one of his bikes."

Kenny gasped.

Chris thought how his friend suddenly looked about ten years old.

"Do you think he would?" Kenny said.

Chris glanced over at Jack, who was leaning on a desk, surrounded by other boys. He looked at least sixteen, and made everyone else look like little kids.

"You're right, Xiao," said Kenny. "I'll go and talk to him."

Chris watched as Kenny walked – no, swaggered, it was definitely a swagger – over to Jack. When he got to the table, the other boys turned to look at him.

"Hi," said Kenny, suddenly looking nervous. "I'm Kenny. I hear you're into motorbikes? I am too."

"Oh really?" said Jack. "Are you sure you mean motorbikes, and not pushbikes?"

The boys around him laughed. This annoyed Chris, as usually those boys were nice to Kenny.

"No, I mean motorbikes," Kenny continued. "I know a load about them. I wondered if you'd like to come around and see my magazine collection."

Chris cringed – what was he doing? This was social suicide.

Jack swept back his hair with his hand. "I think I'll be busy actually riding," he sneered. "But thanks."

Kenny turned and walked back to his friends, the other boys sniggering behind his back as he did.

"He's a total idiot," said Kenny. "I guess looks can be deceiving."

THINKING STORIES

GREAT NIGHT OUT

10

Prepare for the best nights out

The fair was in town, and most children from the local secondary school wanted to go. It was one of the most exciting nights of the year.

At school on Friday afternoon, Lisa and her group of friends were planning their Saturday evening out. They had arranged that Lisa's dad would drop them at the fair at 6pm, and that Amy's mum would collect them again at 10pm. They had spoken to each of their parents and each of them had given their child some money to spend, though two of them had had to do extra chores around the house to earn it. They were all going to make sure their mobile phones were fully charged and that they had coats in case it rained.

Nearby in the playground, two boys, Sam and Charlie, listened in to their conversation. Laughing, they approached the group of girls. "You lot are so sad," said Charlie. "Why not just go to the fair and have a laugh, instead of all this pathetic planning?"

The following evening, Lisa and her friends poured out of her dad's car. The park was transformed into flashing lights, blaring music and massive rides. They started off on the waltzers, screaming in excitement to have their carriage spun faster.

When she climbed off, laughing and with wobbly legs, Lisa caught sight of Sam and Charlie. At first glance, it looked like they were queuing for a ride, but then she realised they were watching the man running it; then as soon as he turned away, they leapt over the bars to further up the line, where the people who had already paid were standing. Lisa felt angry, and hoped that the man would catch them and throw them off. But he didn't, and Sam and Charlie not only managed to skip the queue, but they also got on the ride for free.

Lisa and her friends went on two more rides. They were loving every moment of it. They had just got off the Big Wheel when they saw Sam and Charlie on the Twister ride. They were messing about and trying to stand up in their car as the ride was spinning. A man shouted at them from the side and then the ride had to be stopped. The guy walked up to them and demanded they leave, shouting words such as "dangerous", "idiots", and "get yourselves killed". Sam and Charlie were laughing as they left the ride, and when they got to the steps, Sam did a leap in the air, presumably trying to look cool to all the people who were angry that their ride had been stopped halfway through. The problem was that he misjudged the leap and his foot caught on a step halfway down, causing him to buckle and hit the wooden stairs with a bang. For a second he lay there, clutching his ankle, then Lisa and her friends could hear him start to whimper.

Within seconds, a crowd gathered, and then within minutes an ambulance turned up and took him away. Charlie skulked off home.

Lisa and her friends enjoyed the rest of the fair. They felt bad for Sam, but maybe he wouldn't be so quick to laugh at them next time.

THINKING STORIES

11

Report bullying

Cassie scrolled through her Facebook news feed, smiling at the various photos that her friends had posted of themselves swimming in rivers and posing in front of monuments on holiday.

Additionally, there was the usual array of memes and funny cat videos. Facebook was such a time-waster, but she couldn't seem to help checking it several times a day, usually when she was supposed to be doing her homework.

She scrolled down a little further, and a post caught her eye. A girl in her class, Maxine, had posted a photo of Sara Phillips, a friend of Cassie's, eating a hot dog. It looked like Sara hadn't known the picture was being taken. It wasn't a flattering angle and Sara had her mouth filled with food. Below the picture, Maxine had left a horrible comment, comparing Sara to a pig. She had tagged Sara in the picture.

Cassie thought that Maxine had been very mean, but she wasn't surprised. Maxine was well known for teasing people, particularly other girls who she didn't consider to be "cool" enough. Still, it was none of Cassie's business, and she didn't want to say something and risk Maxine turning on her in the same way. So she closed Facebook and returned to her geography homework.

Later that evening, Cassie checked back in with Facebook. The first post was Maxine's photo of Sara, and there were various new comments underneath it. Cassie opened them up. It seemed that Sara had messaged Maxine privately, asking her to take down the photo, but, instead of doing that, Maxine had posted Sara's message publicly. Lots of people had reacted to that with a laughing symbol.

Cassie opened up her messages and wrote one to Sara: "I've seen the thread. Are you okay?"

Sara replied almost immediately: "Not really. I'm so embarrassed." She put a crying face symbol at the end.

Cassie wrote, "You should tell someone. Your mum?"

Sara wrote, "No, I can't. She worries so much about me anyway. I don't want to make it worse."

Cassie thought for a moment. She opened the whole nasty thread and took a screenshot. Then she emailed it to her school's head teacher, Ms Forbes, explaining what had happened and asking her to please not tell anyone that she had sent it.

The following day, she received an email from Mrs Forbes: "Hi Cassie. Thank you so much for sending me the screenshot. It is thanks to people like you that we as a school can step in and stop bullies. Please rest assured, your involvement in this will remain confidential. Thank you again for setting a good example and being a good friend. Best wishes, Ms Forbes."

THINKING STORIES

> *Do what you feel in your heart to be right—*
>
> *for you'll be criticized anyway.*
>
> -Eleanor Roosevelt

12

Know your strengths – don't be swayed by others

Nebbit was good at swimming. He had always been top of his swimming class since he was at primary school, and now, at age fourteen, he was in the local swimming squad and was captain of his school team.

Football season was coming around again, and Nebbit's friends were all talking about it: what positions they hoped to play this year, which schools they would play against, which they might beat, how many evenings' training they would be able to put in, and so on.

Over lunch, Nebbit's best friend, Simon, turned to him. "Are you going to join this year?"

"He never does," Richard piped up.

"Let the man speak," said Simon.

Nebbit shook his head.

"Ah, come on," said Simon. "You'd be so good at it. You're strong and fast – it'd really help the team if you were there."

"I don't have time," he said.

"Oh right – your precious swimming," said Simon. "You train five nights a week. Is that really necessary?"

Nebbit glared at him. He was so bored of this conversation.

Simon changed tack. He smiled at his friend. "Couldn't you just miss one training a week, to come to football? Surely one evening wouldn't matter, and the season doesn't last long."

Nebbit paused: Simon had a point. "I'll think about it."

The following Thursday, Nebbit turned up at football practice. Simon saw him and ran over to him, fist bumping him and grinning. "Ah, I knew you wouldn't let us down."

KNOW YOUR STRENGTHS

Nebbit grinned back – Simon's enthusiasm was contagious.

The two-hour session was hard but good, and Nebbit undoubtedly did well, despite his inexperience on the pitch. The coach seemed keen for him to come again, which he took to be a good sign. Had Nebbit enjoyed it? Not really.

On his way home, Nebbit got a text from Kate, a friend from his swimming squad. "Are you leaving swimming? Travis said today that anyone who consistently misses training can't stay on the squad. Hope you had a nice evening. We all missed you!"

Nebbit frowned. He didn't think that Travis was serious about that sort of threat, though if he said it again, he may well be.

Nebbit loved swimming. He loved it more than anything, and he wasn't prepared to give it up. Maybe it had been worth trying something new, but he had always known he didn't like football, and tonight hadn't changed his mind. He texted back to Kate: "Of course not. I'll be back tomorrow, and won't be missing sessions again any time soon. I missed you too!"

THINKING STORIES

It is nice to be important, but it is more important to be nice.

13

Treat people kindly

Ricky kicked the ball to his friend, Shiva, and then they and the rest of the group ran up the pitch. Playing football was their favorite thing to do at break time. As he ran, he glanced to the side and saw Jack, the new boy, sitting at the side of the pitch, looking on. He was all alone, eating his packed lunch. He looked sad.

Ricky dropped back from the group, letting them get on with the game without him. He looked at his friends, and then back at Jack. It would be far easier to pretend he hadn't seen him, and get on with his game of football. His group of friends were easy, fun, and he'd known them since he was five. He didn't have to put in much effort around them – they just liked him anyway. But Jack was new, and alone. He didn't know a single person in the school, and Ricky couldn't even imagine what that must feel like.

He sighed, and called out to Shiva, "I'll be back in a minute." Then he turned and walked towards Jack, practicing his most genuine smile as he went.

When Jack saw him approaching, he firstly looked a bit worried, but then relaxed and placed his half-eaten sandwich down in his lunch box.

"Hey," said Ricky. "Jack, isn't it?"

Jack nodded. "And you're Richard?"

Ricky cringed. Some of his teachers called him that, and Jack had obviously heard. "Ricky, actually," he said.

"Oh," said Jack, "Sorry."

"Do you like football?" Ricky asked.

Jack nodded. "I love it, but I'm not that good at it."

"Ah, that doesn't matter," said Ricky. "We're only kicking about. Come and join in?"

Jack smiled, picked up his bag and stood up. Together they went back to the pitch, where Ricky showed Jack to put his stuff next to the goalpost, and then they joined the game.

After school, Ricky and Jack walked home together. It turned out that Jack had just moved into a house only four doors down from him. They chatted all the way, and it turned out they had loads in common.

Treat People Kindly

When Ricky walked through his front door, he felt proud that he had been kind to Jack. Plus, the added bonus was that he had made a great new friend.

Thinking Stories

14

Take time to listen to older people

Robert had never really known his grandad – that is, his dad's dad. He was still alive, but ever since Robert was a baby, he and his parents had lived several hours away from him. Each year they visited him twice, and only for a day at a time.

When Robert was thirteen, his grandad had a fall and needed to stay somewhere with other people around while he recuperated. Robert heard his parents arguing about it in the kitchen.

"Why can't he go into a home?" his mum said.

"He doesn't want to," said his dad.

"But it's only for a few weeks," she said. "You just told me he would be better and ready to go back to his house in a month, maximum."

"Yes, so then why can't he come here?" his dad said.

Robert crept away and went up to his room. He hoped his mum would win the fight. He didn't know his grandad, but what he did know was very boring. He mostly talked about the television, and what the neighbours across the street were building in their garage. Robert wasn't sure that he could handle a month in the same house with that man.

As it turned out, Robert's dad won, and the old man arrived in a taxi the following day. Robert tried to stay out of the way as his dad and the taxi driver helped Grandad into the house and sat him in an armchair by the window. Then Dad called Robert to help lug the suitcases from the car into the dining room, which had been transformed into a downstairs bedroom, as Grandad couldn't manage the stairs.

When Robert came in from school the following day, his Grandad was sitting in the chair, reading the newspaper. His dad had taken the day off work to look after him, and when he saw Robert, he beckoned for him to come into the kitchen.

"Can you watch him for half an hour, son?" he said. "I just need to collect your mum."

Robert wanted to say no, but how could he? He knew he would have to face the boring old man sometime. He walked back to the lounge to prepare himself for a lot of television-talk.

His dad left the house and Robert sat on the sofa, fiddling with his phone.

"How's my grandson?" asked Grandad. He had a habit of referring to Robert in the third person.

"I'm all right," said Robert.

Grandad tried again. "Watched any good soaps recently?"

Here we go, thought Robert. He fought the urge to roll his eyes. "No, I don't really watch TV, Grandad."

"Don't you?"

"No."

Grandad laughed. "Thank God for that!"

Robert looked up.

"I'm so relieved! I would hate my grandson to ruin himself by watching that rubbish. I just thought that's what you kids liked to do."

Robert was confused. "But, isn't it what you like to do?"

"God, no!" said Grandad. "Hate it."

Robert laughed.

Over the next hour, Robert and Grandad talked properly, for probably the first time in Robert's life. He learned all sorts. It turned out Grandad used to work for the United Nations, and over the years he had rescued and liberated hundreds of hostages and refugees around the world.

When Robert's dad came back, Robert wanted him to go back out again. How had he never known all this about his grandfather? Why hadn't his father told him that he was the most interesting person who ever lived? Robert considered being angry with his father, but he knew deep down that the reason he didn't know his grandfather was because he had avoided speaking to him for the last fourteen years.

While Robert wished more than anything that his grandad had not had a fall, in some ways it had proved to be a blessing.

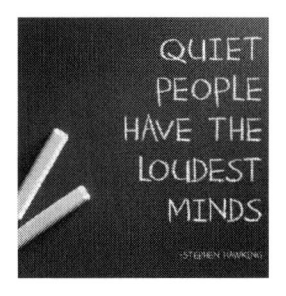

15

Those who shout loudest aren't always right

Mrs Winters was excited about the new term. She had a brand-new English class to teach, and from what she could see on day one, they were a lively group.

To get the ball rolling, and to enable herself to get to know her new students more quickly, she started her first session by introducing some controversial topics for discussion. She went through some of the more obvious, fairly provocative subjects such as fox hunting and gun laws.

Very quickly, she picked up that there were five students who were particularly outspoken and instantly shouted their opinions on whatever was being discussed. Many more students contributed every now and then. There was one student, however, that didn't utter a word, or raise her hand. She was

61

small and sat halfway back, on the left against the wall.

Mrs Winters moved onto the next topic on the list: euthanasia. Instantly, the class erupted into a lively debate, with most students joining in to some degree. Each of the loudest students had a very strong opinion one way or the other. She noticed, however, that the student on the left still hadn't contributed. Over the years, Mrs Winters had seen students like this: they often couldn't be bothered, or they weren't even listening. However, she could see that this girl was different. She appeared to be following everything that was going on, occasionally frowning ever so slightly when a classmate said something particularly aggressive.

Intrigued, Mrs Winters hushed the class and addressed this girl directly. "I'm sorry – what's your name?"

The girl's eyes widened, and for a few seconds Mrs Winters regretted her decision to pick on her; she looked terrified.

"Shannon Pike," said the girl.

Mrs Winters nodded. "And what's your opinion on euthanasia, Shannon?"

The class fell silent. A few of the louder students nudged each other and sniggered.

"I think that with something as complex as euthanasia, it is difficult to form a full opinion without properly considering it from all angles."

Mrs Winters tilted her head to one side. "Isn't that what we are doing today? Does listening to your classmates' opinions not help you form your own?"

Shannon maintained strong eye contact. "No, because I don't think anyone in this room is qualified to really know all about it."

"Okay," said Mrs Winters. She was starting to like Shannon. "So, if I asked you to write a research paper about it, stating your opinion at the end, that would be better?"

Shannon smiled. "Much better."

"Fine," she said, and then turned to the whole class. "That's what I want you all to do, by this Friday."

There was a series of groans from around the room, except for Shannon, who dutifully made a note in her diary.

As Mrs Winters left the classroom, she reflected on the importance of listening to every opinion, not just of those who shout the loudest.

THINKING STORIES

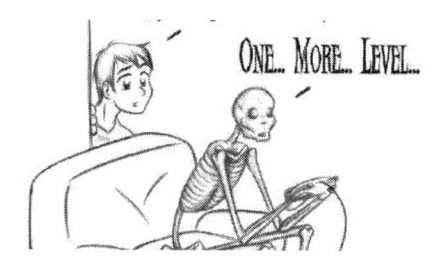

16

Everything in moderation

Rasheed entered a school raffle and won a lesson at the local skiing school. He was thrilled – he had never been skiing before.

He turned up at his lesson, put on the kit and the big heavy boots, and got started. He loved every minute.

As soon as he got home, he told his mum all about it and announced that he was going to visit the ski slope the following day after school, to really get into his practice.

He kept to his word, and spent all of the next evening skiing. In fact, he went the next two evenings as well, and then all day on Saturday. By Sunday, of course, he was in a lot of pain. His whole body ached, but especially his thighs. By Monday, he had decided that he was clearly no good at skiing, and swore never to go again.

The following month, Rasheed visited his cousin's house and played on his games console. Within a couple of hours, he was hooked. He tried out a few games, but the war game was his favourite. He enjoyed coming up with complex strategies and then working with his computer team to implement them.

The next day, Rasheed looked online and found a second-hand console for sale. A boy down the road had upgraded to a new model and so was selling his old one cheap. Rasheed jumped at the opportunity and took his birthday money round to purchase it.

He got the console home and set it up in his bedroom, where he didn't leave it for the rest of the weekend. On Monday, he went to school, but all he could think about was getting home to play the war game. He stayed up all Monday night playing it. He was getting pretty good now, and had progressed several levels. On Tuesday, he was tired, and had to drink several coffees before school to be able to even pretend to listen.

The week carried on like this, and by Friday he was so tired he couldn't even go to school. He just sat at the kitchen table, staring into his breakfast cereal.

His dad sat down next to him. "I think you need to move the console into the lounge, son," he said. "You have to start sleeping at night, otherwise you will start to struggle at school."

Rasheed looked at his father. "You're right," he said. "But other people manage to play games and still do well at school."

"I very much doubt that they stay up all night," he replied.

"I think I'm just not very good at gaming," Rasheed said.

That evening, he boxed up his console and his games, and stored them all under his bed.

At dinner, he felt sad. "What's wrong with me, Dad?" he said. "I don't seem to be good at anything."

His father looked confused. "What are you talking about?" he said. "You are good at so many things."

Rasheed shook his head. "I'm no good at skiing, or gaming. And last month I also discovered that I'm not good at swimming, or creative writing, or computer coding."

"That is absolutely not true," his father said. "You excelled at each and every one of those things. The problem is that you burnt yourself out with them. You need to learn to do things in moderation."

"Moderation?" said Rasheed, as if it were a word he'd never heard before. "How?"

His dad smiled. "You could do skiing once a week, then your legs wouldn't hurt. You could play on your console, but go to sleep by midnight." He looked at his son with real affection. "It's not rocket science, Rasheed. Though, of course, even with rocket science, you'd have to pace yourself."

Make sure the important **PEOPLE** *in your* **LIFE** *know they are important before it's too late*

17

Respect people's time

Sinead was often late. She was late for school, for lessons, for meeting friends. In short, she was late for almost everything. Usually her lateness was around twenty minutes, but sometimes it was half an hour, or even an hour. The problem was, of course, that everyone was getting annoyed with it.

One Saturday, Sinead was supposed to meet her friend, Joanne, outside the cinema for a movie that was starting at 11.30am. Sinead took a little longer in the shower than she meant to, and then as she was about to leave the house, she flicked through a magazine and saw an interesting article, so sat down to read it. After that, she couldn't find her house keys, and so had to spend ten minutes hunting around for them.

By the time she arrived at the cinema, Joanne looked angry. "You're forty minutes late," she said. "The film's already started."

"We've only missed the beginning," said Sinead. "It doesn't matter."

Joanne glared at her. "It matters to me!" She turned away. "I'll go and see it tomorrow, with someone else."

Sinead watched as Joanne walked away down the road. She had only been a bit late, she thought, and she had good reason. It could happen to anyone.

The following Sunday, Sinead had been invited to her friend Rachel's house for lunch. She had told her they were eating at 1.30pm, and her mother was cooking a roast dinner.

On the day, Sinead went to the shops in the morning, and got a little distracted trying on shoes and winter coats. The weather was starting to get cold and she knew it was vital that she got some warm and waterproof clothes to wear. Therefore, when she checked her phone and saw that it was already 1.15pm, she figured she could afford to be a little late, as this was so important. She went to another three shops, to make sure she was making the right choice, before returning to the first shop for the shoes and coat.

At 2.45pm, Sinead knocked on Rachel's door.

Respect People's Time

Rachel answered it, and then came out onto the doorstep, closing the door behind her. "Where were you? My mum's furious," she hissed.

"I got tied up," said Sinead. "I'm sorry. Can we just heat up the food a bit?"

"We've all eaten," said Rachel. After half an hour, we figured you weren't coming. I tried to ring you three times."

"Sorry," said Sinead.

"Well, it's too late now," said Rachel. "You'd better go."

Over the next two months, Sinead lost each and every one of her friends in this way. They were still nice to her when they saw her, but no one invited her to do anything with them any more, and if she suggested something, they all made excuses. She knew from Facebook that they were all still meeting up and doing fun things together.

One day, she asked Joanne what was going on. "I'm sorry I was late for the cinema. I know it's annoying. I can work on that."

Joanne sighed. "It isn't really about the lateness, exactly," she said. "You don't seem to realise that no one wants to stand around waiting for you for half an hour – they have better things to be getting on with. The problem is that you don't respect people's time."

71

As she watched Joanne walk away for the second time in as many months, Sinead knew that she was right.

> NEVER BE AFRAID TO TRY SOMETHING NEW, BECAUSE LIFE GETS BORING WHEN YOU STAY WITHIN THE LIMITS OF WHAT YOU ALREADY KNOW

18

Try new things – you might discover a new talent

Masood was reasonable at school. She was very good at some things – mainly maths and science – and not good at other things – such as painting and literature. She had got used to these facts and had accepted them, but it always hurt a little when someone commented on how poor her drawing was, or that she had completely missed the point of a poem. Her way of coping with this was to avoid doing those things as much as she possibly could.

Activities week came around, and she carefully selected options that wouldn't embarrass her. On the Monday, she went into school feeling optimistic. She had chosen computer coding for the morning, and wildlife studies for the afternoon. However, when she got to form, her tutor announced that the coding teacher had been taken ill, and so the group would be doing sculpture instead.

Masood was annoyed and worried, in equal measures. She was rubbish at art and, besides, how was sculpture even slightly similar to coding?! Still, she wasn't a difficult student, so she went along to the class, prepared to be humiliated.

A woman introduced herself as Kelly and explained that she was a sculptor and that she mainly carved wood. She showed the class some of her pieces, including an owl, a horse, and a person.

She handed out a piece of wood and a knife to every student. Masood decided to get the shame out of the way. When Kelly came to her, she said, "I'm really not good at art."

"Art is a massive term," Kelly said, smiling. "No-one is bad at *all* forms."

"I am," said Masood.

"Have you tried wood-carving?" she said.

"Well, no, but…"

"Give it a try," Kelly said, placing the wood and knife down in front of her. "You might surprise yourself."

Masood sat and stared at the task ahead. She sighed, and picked up the knife. She knew she needed to do

Try New Things

something, even if it was going to be awful. She looked at the piece of wood. The way it was curved made it look like some sort of fish. Maybe she could do a dolphin. Slowly, she used the knife to carve away some of the wood at the end, to shape a tail. At first it didn't look anything like one, but after she had carved away several pieces, methodically, it started to take shape.

At the end of the class, she had basically made a dolphin. It wasn't perfect, but Kelly came over and held it up for the rest of the class as a good example of a wood carving! Masood was shocked, but when she looked around at her classmates' attempts, she could see that hers really was pretty good.

As she left the class for lunch, she smiled at Kelly and thanked her. Had she not been forced into trying it, she never would have found that she had a hidden talent.

THINKING STORIES

> Don't judge me until
> you know me,
> Don't underestimate me until
> you challenge me and
> Don't talk about me until
> you've talked to me.

19

Be yourself – don't always try to fit in

Caroline pulled on her trainers, silently cursing herself for not coming up with a good reason to be excused from hockey. She hated P.E., mainly because her tallness was even more apparent during this class than it was the rest of the time. A good foot taller than any of her classmates, she couldn't bend down easily to hit the hockey ball. Plus, she was always tripping over her own feet, which, of course, were larger than those of all of her friends. In other classes, she tried to sit down as much as possible or, if she had to stand, she tried to stoop, or lean against something, to appear shorter and more normal. But in P.E. Caroline felt like a clumsy, awkward giant.

She glumly followed the rest of the girls out of the changing room and onto the playground where Ms Grace, the P.E. teacher, was waiting for them.

"Right, everyone," she boomed, "the hockey field is waterlogged from all the rain, so we're going to do some basketball instead."

Caroline's heart sank even further. Basketball was another sport she'd never tried and that was bound to make her look like a buffoon. She walked over towards the basketball courts.

"Cheer up, Caroline," said Ms Grace, "I think you'll enjoy this."

Caroline doubted it.

The class was split into teams. Ms Grace briefly explained the rules, and off they went.

In just fifteen minutes, Caroline had earned a whopping twenty-four points for her team. She was light-heartedly deemed a heroine.

Afterwards, Caroline asked Ms Grace, "How did you know I'd do well?"

Ms Grace said, "Watch some basketball on television tonight. Successful players are very often taller than average. With your height and skill, you have the potential to be a very good player."

Be Yourself

Caroline walked back to the changing room, a new spring in her step. Maybe being her wasn't so bad after all.

THINKING STORIES

> MISTAKES
> are the
> stepping stones
> TO Learning!

20

Don't be afraid to admit mistakes

Sanjay had finally convinced his mum to let him have a key to their house. He had been trying to talk her into it for a good year, and when she finally handed it to him on his twelfth birthday, he was so pleased. It meant that she trusted him to be there on his own (admittedly only for short periods of time) and that he could come straight home from school, rather than having to go to an after-school club until she finished work.

Another added bonus was that he didn't have to go into school early any more. This Monday morning was Sanjay's first morning with his new key. He waved his mum off at 8am and then settled onto the sofa to watch TV while eating his breakfast.

At 8.45am, Sanjay left the house and walked to school. He arrived by 8.55, in perfect time, all according to plan. He went to registration and then off to his first lesson.

He had just sat down at his maths desk when he suddenly remembered something awful: he hadn't locked the front door. Sanjay's heart raced. His mum was going to be so angry. She had gone on and on about the importance of securing the house, and it was actually one of the reasons she hadn't wanted to give him his own key for so long. More important, of course, was the worry that someone could walk into the house and take all of their possessions. Sanjay wasn't really in the know about house insurance rules, but he was fairly sure that if you left your house unlocked and open for any old burglar, the insurance wouldn't pay out.

What was he going to do? He could ring his mum, but then she would be angry and take his key away. So, he could keep quiet and hope for the best, but then what if the house did get burgled? The police would see that the lock hadn't been broken, and then he would be found out anyway.

Sanjay sat sweating all through maths. He couldn't concentrate on anything; he was just thinking about his unlocked house and his shiny silver key that wouldn't be in his pocket for much longer.

DON'T BE AFRAID TO ADMIT MISTAKES

At the end of the class, Miss Sleamon approached him. "Whatever's the matter, Sanjay?" she said. "You look terrible."

Sanjay took a breath and told her the whole story.

Once he had finished, Miss Sleamon smiled at him. "Listen, the chances are that everything is fine, but it is really important that we do something about this. An unlocked house is, as you say, at risk. Do you have a neighbour that has a key?"

Of course! Mr Giles, their next-door neighbour. Why didn't Sanjay think of that before? Quickly, he pulled out his mobile phone, rang Mr Giles, and asked him to please go around and lock the house for him. Mr Giles agreed and told Sanjay not to worry – he would do it immediately.

When Sanjay put his phone away, he was so relieved he wanted to hug Miss Sleamon. He resisted, though. "I'm so glad I admitted my mistake," he said. "I wish I'd done it sooner."

Thinking Stories

Money isn't everything

21

Don't judge people by money or possessions

Melissa jogged to catch up with her friend, Cathy. She liked it when they walked home from school together as they lived just one street apart. Plus, Cathy was always so lovely and fun to talk to.

As they walked through down the hill away from the school, Melissa said, "We have to bring in donations for the food bank tomorrow, don't we?"

Cathy nodded.

"What even is a food bank?" said Melissa. "Obviously I know it's a place for poor people to get free food, but I've never seen one. Do you think it's like a shop, but with no money?"

Cathy laughed. "I don't think it's quite like that," she said. "I think they are usually in a town hall side-room."

Melissa thought for a minute. "Okay, yes, that makes sense," she said. "You'd have to be pretty desperate though, wouldn't you, to admit you don't even have five pounds for some food, and that you need to scrounge off everyone else. Come to think of it, I don't believe that anyone truly has no money, at least not around here."

Cathy turned to look at her as they walked. "What do you mean, 'around here'?"

Melissa shrugged. "Well, it's quite a rich area, isn't it?"

"It doesn't always mean anything," she said.

Cathy didn't say much after that, so Melissa changed the subject and rabbited on about school and how she couldn't wait to not have to do French any more when they chose their options next year. Cathy answered politely but wasn't her normal self for the rest of the journey, and eventually they parted company and both went to their own houses.

About two weeks later, on a Saturday, Melissa had walked into town to buy some new shoes. She passed the town hall and saw Cathy coming out, carrying a box.

"Hey Cathy," Melissa said, walking up to her. She was pleased to see her. "What's in the box?"

Cathy took a deep breath. "It's food."

Don't Judge People by Money or Possessions

"Food?" said Melissa.

"Yes," Cathy replied. "From the food bank."

Melissa nodded. She didn't know what to say, but she felt an awful ache in her stomach that she knew was guilt.

"Since Dad died, Mum has really struggled to support us," said Cathy. "There are some weeks that we can't even have the heating on. The food bank has been a lifesaver."

"But you always seem so neat and lovely," said Melissa.

Cathy laughed. "Just because we have no money doesn't mean we don't have pride."

THINKING STORIES

> It's simple..
> Never lie to someone who trusts you,
> and never trust someone who lies to you..

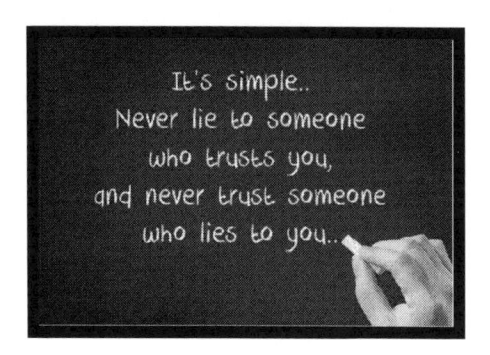

22

Not everyone tells the truth

Sanjay lived in a quiet neighbourhood, and a new neighbour had just moved in next door. He seemed to work long hours and always wore smart business suits. Sanjay often saw him when he came home in the evenings. He would park his car in the driveway, get out of his silver Porsche, and take his briefcase inside. He often whistled, or hummed, as he did so. He seemed so happy. Sanjay wanted a lifestyle like that when he finished school.

One day, Sanjay arrived home from school to see his neighbour in his driveway, washing his Porsche. It was the first time Sanjay had known him to have a day off during the week. The car was gleaming, and Sanjay stopped to admire it.

The man, crouched beside the wheel, looked up at him. "Would you like to have a look around it?" he said.

Sanjay grinned. "Yes please, Mr…"

"It's Mike," said the man, standing up and wiping his wet hand off on his jeans. He held it out to Sanjay. "And you are?"

"Sanjay," he said, accepting Mike's handshake. "Nice to meet you."

Sanjay followed Mike to the Porsche, where he opened the driver's door and let Sanjay sit in it and start up the engine.

Sanjay loved cars, but he had never even sat in a Porsche before, let alone been allowed to *touch stuff*. Mike sat in the passenger's seat and told him all about the car, using all sorts of technical terms that Sanjay was too embarrassed to admit he didn't understand, so he just smiled and nodded along.

When they got out of the car, Sanjay turned to Mike. "What's your job?" he asked.

"I work for the Prime Minister," he said.

Sanjay's eyes widened. "Wow," he said. "What sort of work?"

"I can't go into details, I'm afraid, Sanjay," he said. "Security reasons. I'm sure you understand?"

"Oh yes, of course," said Sanjay, trying to hide his disappointment.

"Well, feel free to come over and work on the car with me some time," Mike said. "I'll even take you for a ride, if you like."

"Yes please!" said Sanjay.

Sanjay thanked Mike for letting him sit in the Porsche, then he headed back to his own house, thinking how perfect Mike's life was. Working for the Prime Minister sounded like a great way to earn money.

Over the next week, Sanjay kept hoping to see Mike and take him up on his car offer, but he didn't see him at all.

One day, Sanjay came home from school to see the Porsche gone, and a "For sale" sign up outside the house. From what he could see through the windows, the house was completely empty.

He went inside where his dad was working at the computer. "What happened to Mike?" said Sanjay.

His dad looked up. "Mike?"

"Mike from next door. With the Porsche…?" Sanjay said.

"Oh, the police got him." His dad turned back to the screen. "Drug trafficking. About time too."

"I thought he worked for the prime minister," said Sanjay, quietly.

His dad looked back at him. Was that pity in his eyes? "Just because someone wears a flash suit and drives a Porsche," he said, "doesn't mean they're telling the truth."

Words Can
HURT
or
HEAL
What Did Yours Do Today?

23

If people gossip to you, they probably gossip about you as well

Laura had sprained her ankle and so wasn't able to take part in P.E. for a couple of weeks. Being a healthy person, she had never missed it before, and so she felt a little out of her depth as she sat on a bench at the side of the playground with three other girls who, for various reasons, were also excused from taking part. Laura didn't know them very well, but they often seemed to be off P.E.

As soon as she sat down, she could hear that the three of them were talking about Cassie, another girl in their class.

"She has the fattest legs," said Jessie, the meanest of the three girls. "I don't know how she can be seen out in public wearing that skirt."

Laura remained silent. All the girls had the same uniform – everyone wore the same skirt. Besides, Cassie didn't have fat legs, and even if she did, who cared?! Still, she didn't want to get on the wrong side of these girls – they were really popular – so she pretended not to be listening, and watched the P.E lesson taking place.

The next day followed much the same pattern. When it was time for P.E., Laura sat down on the bench, next to two of the girls, Jessie and one other.

Jessie slid across so that she was sitting very close to Laura, leaned in towards her conspiratorially, and said, "What do you think about Sanna? Did you *see* how much she ate at lunch today? Disgusting!"

Laura's heart raced. She had never even been acknowledged by the popular girls before, let alone spoken to. Sanna was a nice enough girl but it's true that she did like her food, and everyone knew about it. Laura was torn between defending Sanna, and being liked by Jessie. Eventually, she said, "I know – what a gross pig!" and she laughed a fake laugh. She hated the sound of it.

"Exactly!" said Jessie, and draped her arm around Laura's shoulders.

IF PEOPLE GOSSIP TO YOU...

Laura smiled. Could this be the moment that the cool group finally accepted her?

For the next half an hour, Laura and Jessie talked and laughed about various people in the school. After a while, Laura stopped feeling bad about it. After all, she had friends now, so who cared?

The following day, when Laura came into school and into her form room, no one would speak to her. All the girls grouped together and when she approached, they stared at her and then walked off. The same thing happened in all of her morning lessons. Eventually, Cassie came up to her.

"It looks like you can't understand why no-one likes you," she said.

Laura shook her head, trying not to cry. "No…"

"Jessie told everyone all the mean things you've been saying," she said, and then she laughed a bit. "I'm actually surprised that someone as clever as you made the mistake of trusting Jessie and her harem."

"I… I'm sorry," Laura stuttered.

Cassie shrugged and walked away, leaving Laura standing on her own.

THINKING STORIES

> HURT ME WITH THE TRUTH
> BUT NEVER
> COMFORT ME WITH A LIE

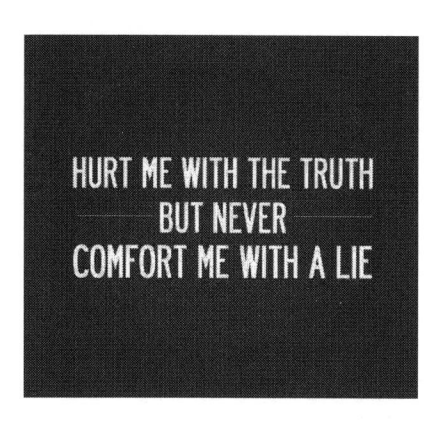

24

Don't invent things to get attention

It was Ashley's first day at his new school, and he didn't know anyone. His teacher showed him where to sit, and he was surrounded by other students who all messed around and joked like they'd known each other forever.

For the morning, he barely spoke to anyone; he just kept his head down and got on with his work. However, he was jealous of all the fun they were having, and he desperately wanted to make friends. At lunch time, a group of boys were talking about quad bikes. One of their fathers had just bought one, apparently, and they were all planning when they could go around to his farm to try it out.

Ashley wanted to be invited. He thought fast. "I've got one of those," he piped up.

The boys stopped talking and looked at him. "A quad bike?" said the tallest one – his name was Soumi.

Ashley swallowed. He had never even sat on a quad bike, let alone owned one. "Yes," he continued. "I've had one for ages. I can do tricks on it and everything."

Another of the boys grinned. "Cool," he said. "Can I have a go?"

Ashley froze for a second. They were all staring at him. He nodded. "Yep, okay."

This seemed to work. They invited him to have lunch with them and then they all talked to him throughout the rest of the day, mainly about his quad bike.

The following day, Ashley got into school, hoping they'd be discussing the same thing, though of course worrying about what would happen when they really pushed to come over and ride his quad bike. However, when he got there, the group were busy discussing computer games. Three of them had the latest consoles and were exchanging tips about the new war game. Ashley didn't have a console. He wanted one, but his mum said the games were too violent.

"Oh, I'm getting that game on Saturday," said Ashley.

Don't Invent Things to Get Attention

Once again, all the boys looked at him, interested.

"That's great," one of them said. "We can play together online. I'll give you my ID so you can find me."

"Okay, great," said Ashley, smiling.

The rest of the week went well. Ashley now had a proper group of friends to hang out with. However, his pride was short-lived.

That Sunday, Ashley was celebrating having got through his first week by having a super-long lie in. At about 11am, he heard the doorbell ring, and his mum walked through the hallway to answer it.

He froze as he heard familiar voices – it was the boys from school. Ashley leapt out of bed and frantically pulled on his clothes over his pyjamas. He needed to get down there straight away.

He opened his bedroom door and got to the top of the stairs just as he heard his mum laugh and say, "War games? Ashley isn't allowed that sort of thing!"

Oh no. He tried to get down the stairs quickly, while still pretending to be relaxed. "Hi guys!" he said.

They all looked up at him.

Soumi frowned. "I'll bet you don't have a quad bike either," he said.

99

Ashley opened his mouth to speak, but he didn't know what to say so he paused, which allowed his mum time to say, "Of course not! Where would we keep something like that, in this house?"

Soumi nodded slowly. He looked disappointed. "See you around, Ashley," he said.

The group left, closing the front door behind them. Ashley turned and walked back to his bedroom.

Compliment PEOPLE, Magnify their STRENGTHS, Not their weaknesses.

25

Be patient with others

Bella had just got a new games console for her birthday. It was all she had asked for as she so wanted it. Her friend Simone had one and was always talking about it. Simone had told Bella that if she had one, they could chat on their headphones while playing the same games at their own houses. Bella was sold on this idea.

Her mum spent an hour setting it up with her and then Bella texted Simone to say she was online, and would she like to play?

Within minutes, Simone appeared online and sent her a friend request. Soon they were chatting on their headphones, just as Bella had dreamed.

THINKING STORIES

Simone invited Bella into her favourite game. Bella accepted and found herself in a world where she had to build structures and try to survive against a series of monsters and other hazards. Of course, she didn't even know how to use the controls yet.

"How do you build things?" she asked Simone.

"Oh, use the middle button," she replied.

"Which middle button?"

Simone didn't answer. She was chatting and laughing with someone else.

Bella fiddled around with the controller and figured out how to lay a few basic blocks. Progress.

Suddenly, a monster came out of nowhere. "Agh, Simone, I'm getting attacked!" she said.

"God, Bella," Simone snapped. "If I'd known you were this useless, I wouldn't have suggested you got the console."

Bella's face fell. Simone was right – she was useless. She logged out, turned off the console, and went to her bedroom in tears.

A minute later, there was a knock at her bedroom door and her mum came in. "What happened?" she said, sitting down on the edge of Bella's bed.

Bella sat up and explained.

BE PATIENT WITH OTHERS

"You don't need to cry about some silly girl," said her mum. "Everyone has to learn. Simone would have had to learn to begin with, too."

"Yes, I suppose so," said Bella.

Her mum thought for a moment. "Your cousin Josh plays that game. I'll see if he's around to give you a crash course."

Within the hour, Josh was at the front door, smiling at Bella when she opened it. He held up his own headphones and controller. "Let's get started," he said.

For the rest of the afternoon, Bella and Josh played on her new console. He patiently taught her which controls did what, and how to access different parts of the game. Soon, Bella was getting pretty fast.

Suddenly, Simone appeared online again. This time, Bella invited her to come into her game. She accepted and entered the world.

"Who built all this?" said Simone through the headphones.

"Me and Josh," said Bella. Bella knew Simone would be jealous – she had a crush on Josh.

"Oh, right," she said. "I bet he did all the work, though."

103

"Actually, Bella did most of it," Josh said. (Simone didn't know he was still there and could hear her.) "Once I'd taken the time to show her the controls, she was fine. That's what proper friends do," he said.

Bella grinned as she heard Simone stuttering for what to say. In the end, she logged out, and Bella and Josh spent the rest of the day playing games.

26
Be kind to animals

Sanja never really understood why his friends had pets. "They are just dumb animals," he'd say. "Why not just hang out with people instead?" Of course, his comments provoked some strong responses from his classmates. Ben, for example, had a cat, that he said he loved more than his own brother. Katrina had a hamster and a dog, both of whom slept in her bedroom at night. But Sanjay always shook his head a little, though perhaps not visibly, when he heard them talking about their pets.

Then one day, the school organised a trip to a local riding school. The idea was that students could learn a little about the horses, and about the task of keeping them in good health and fitness, so that they could help customers who wished to learn to ride. Sanjay dutifully went along with the class, though he was

105

mainly looking forward to avoiding normal lessons for a morning.

When they arrived, a young woman called Maya met the class and led them into the stable yard. She walked along a line of stables, introducing the class to several horses, all of whom had their heads sticking out over their doors, happy to meet everyone. By the third, Sanjay was bored. He almost wished he was back in normal school. The next, however, was to change everything.

The fourth stable in the row didn't have a horse looking out of it. Maya explained that this horse, Casper, had only been with them for a week. Casper had been poorly treated in the past and was still shy. A few of Sanjay's friends peered over the door and made clicking sounds, but he wasn't convinced to come forward.

As Maya and the rest of the class moved on to the next stable, Sanjay was curious about Casper, so he lingered and peered into the gloom. He could see a silver horse, with black spots on its rump. Sanjay could see that he was magnificent; his muscles were taut, and his coat gleamed. As Maya had said, however, Casper was clearly shy. He stared at Sanjay with wild eyes, their whites showing around the edges.

Something about this horse made Sanjay want to keep looking at him, to stay with him. He looked at the horse as his eyes rolled and his nostrils flared, and Sanjay thought, *I won't hurt you. You can trust me.*

BE KIND TO ANIMALS

Sanjay didn't know why he was thinking these things, but to his astonishment, Casper snorted gently, and then, very slowly, walked towards the door. Sanjay didn't move, in case he frightened the poor thing. When Casper reached him, he lifted his head and put his muzzle to Sanjay's face. Sanjay chuckled, though as quietly as possible so as not to startle him. He felt the warm breath on his face, and then Casper retreated again, though only by a step, and continued to watch him. His eyes looked calmer.

Suddenly remembering where he was, Sanjay glanced to the side. Maya and the whole class were watching him in bewilderment.

Maya smiled. "I've not seen him get that close to anyone," she said. "He must know you're a kind person. You should come back and see him again…"

Sanjay allowed himself to smile back, and when he looked again at Casper, he knew he would be back, just as soon as he could.

Thinking Stories

Testimonials:

"I have known Nadine for many years now as my French tutor and as a good friend. Her passion for children's issues and literature during that time has consistently shone. Her book is a culmination of years of hard work and patience and is the perfect antidote for children in modern times. The stories relate to all manner of challenges children face on a day-to-day basis. They are a very enjoyable read and I am sure will have a positive influence on all who read them. I wish Nadine all the best of luck with this and future publications. Her stories are heartfelt, as is her concern for the struggles many young people face."
Neil Everden

"The topics that inspired Nadine Webb are current and relevant to most children nowadays from 7 to 20 years old. They are short, to the point and give hope or guidance in a subtle way. I really enjoyed reading them and thoroughly recommend this book to anyone who has, or works with, children."
Mohamed Ghediri

"I am not surprised that Nadine has published this book; she has never liked to see children suffer and if she had the money she would help all the orphans of the world. In her own way she manages to touch our mind and our heart, and I can only recommend this book which comes from a deep and loving place."
Martine Fdida

Thanks to:

My daughter Alexis for her constant support regarding formatting or technical problems; my many friends who think my book will help children; Christopher Payne (http://www.christopherjohnpayne.com) for his advice and support to authors; and numerous pupils over the years, who were incredible, genuine, generous, inspiring and deeply caring.

One final thing…

I would appreciate if you would review my book on Amazon. Also, you can drop me a line or ask me any questions, including suggestions of topics for new stories, by emailing me at nadinefrance22@gmail.com.

Printed in Poland
by Amazon Fulfillment
Poland Sp. z o.o., Wrocław